Facing the ACTS

TWENTY-EIGHT DAYS TO EXPERIENCE MIRACLES, SIGNS & WONDERS

YOLANDA PERRY

DEDICATION

To My Expecting GREATER Crew.
This journey began and ended with you.
From announcing the baby to come,
watching it grow, and giving it a name.
Thank you for sharing this experience with me!

CONTENTS

INTRODUCTION

The Book of Acts is indeed one of my favorites in the Bible. I have read through it many times, in many different versions. Finally, this time I decided to share my own personal insights as I journeyed through it once more.

This book serves to fuel your faith and encourage you in your Christian walk. I hope that you realize from each day's devotions, you are challenged to not just be an ordinary Christian.

You are called to do more.
You are called to be more.
You are called to have more.
You are called to say more.
You are called to see more.
You are called to expect more.

You are called to a life marked by miracles, signs and wonders. May this book encourage, provoke, and even ignite a fire to be one who moves in all three on a daily basis. Let each day's devotions cause you to be so stirred that you decide that you are without excuse and that you must move in that measure of God's power as though it is the norm.

DAY ONE:
PERFECT TIMING

Jesus said to them, "The times and occasions are set by my Father's own authority, and it is not for you to know when they will be.
~Acts 1:7 (GNT)

AFFIRMATION
Today...I will trust that God knows exactly when to show up on my behalf.

JUST A THOUGHT

Oftentimes we are in a hurry for God to move in our circumstances based upon how we view them in a given moment. Time is of the essence for a person who is in a race against the clock because of a deadline that is attached to potential financial demise; a sickness that has the potential to claim a loved one's life; or even a wayward child that appears to be headed toward destruction and needs salvation now. It is during times like these that we cry out to God and become desperate, expressing our need for Him to move "NOW". For Holy Spirit to show up "NOW". From time to time, many even slip into the predicting game, attempting to determine that breakthrough is coming based on where things stand. However, we ought not ever waste time fretting about His timing concerning anything. As the Scripture says, we do not know exactly when God—Holy Spirit—will come to our rescue. We simply need to know that He will.

PRAYER

Lord...May I always trust the timing of your perfect will to be made manifest in my life. In Jesus' name, Amen.

DAY TWO:
MIRACLES ARE IN YOU TOO

'This is what I will do in the last days', God says: I will pour out my Spirit on everyone. Your sons and daughters will proclaim my message; your young men will see visions, and your old men will have dreams. Yes, even on my servants, both men and women, I will pour out my Spirit in those days, and they will proclaim my message. I will perform miracles in the sky above and wonders on the earth below...'
~Acts 2:17-19a (GNT)

Many miracles and wonders were being done through the apostles, and everyone was filled with awe.
~Acts 2:43 (GNT)

AFFIRMATION
Today...The Spirit of God is in full operation in my life; and I expect miracles to flow through me!

<u>JUST A THOUGHT</u>

Oftentimes, many are filled with wonder and are mesmerized by the gifts of the Holy Spirit that operates through certain people. Every now and then the next prophetic wonder or the next miracle worker rises up. Everyone stops and takes notice. The chatter of how great God is using them gets louder and louder and louder. Is this an issue? Not really. Yet, it could be. The problem is found in the fact that many doubt whether they could be used in such capacity as well. For the record, you can. There are miracles, signs and wonders locked on the inside of you too. Unlock, activate and release them!

<u>PRAYER</u>

Lord...May I flow and function in every gift You so generously bestowed upon me. In Jesus' name, Amen.

DAY THREE:
THE JESUS IN YOU

When Peter saw the people, he said to them, "Fellow Israelites, why are you surprised at this, and why do you stare at us? Do you think that it was by means of our own power or godliness that we made this man walk?
~Acts 3:12 (GNT)

It was the power of his name that gave strength to this lame man. What you see and know was done by faith in his name; it was faith in Jesus that has made him well, as you can all see.
~Acts 3:16 (GNT)

AFFIRMATION
Today...I am confidently relying on the One who lives in me to make things happen.

JUST A THOUGHT

On a daily basis, we walk by those in need with compassion, hoping and praying they will be healed, delivered, rescued from their misery. More often than not, we do not take a moment to simply offer them what we have...the Jesus whose living on the inside of us. What if that is all it would take for a little boy who rolled into the department store in a wheelchair? What if that is all it would take for that young man who walked past you in the mall, headed home to take his own life? What if that is all it would take to lead the homeless man on the park bench to salvation? The Jesus living on the inside of you no longer wants to be bored, hanging out in hiding. He likes action; which will happen when you begin to release and unleash Him to those who need Him.

PRAYER

Lord...Please give me the boldness to present you to those who are in need of an encounter with you. In Jesus' name, Amen.

DAY FOUR:
FROM REJECTED
TO RESPECTED

Jesus is the one of whom the scripture says, 'The stone that you the builders despised turned out to be the most important of all.'
~Acts 4:11 (GNT)

AFFIRMATION

Today...I will be seen for who I am in Him, not for my past or limitations that people perceive I have.

<u>JUST A THOUGHT</u>

Everyone is judged by the naked eye at one time or another. Sometimes based on the reality of a person's current status, what people perceive could even seem justified. Most will set a person's value at what they can see of them right now, not ever considering what God has in store for that very person in the future. Take my own life, for example, many would consider my past as one that would guarantee a future of doom and gloom. They called that all wrong. Many are counted out just the same, just like Jesus was. But as with Jesus, who was rejected, so shall you become the one who is not only accepted but also respected.

<u>PRAYER</u>

Lord...May my tarnished reputation be restored, my name be cleared and my value be reset based on my life in You. In Jesus' name, Amen.

DAY FIVE:
GRACE TO ENDURE

They called the apostles in, had them whipped, and ordered them never again to speak in the name of Jesus; and then they set them free. As the apostles left the Council, they were happy, because God had considered them worthy to suffer disgrace for the sake of Jesus. And every day in the Temple and in people's homes they continued to teach and preach the Good News about Jesus the Messiah.
~Acts 5:40-42 (GNT)

<u>AFFIRMATION</u>

Today...I will not consider the consequence or cost; I will obey God no matter what.

JUST A THOUGHT

So often people are silent about the things of God because they are concerned about how others will feel or how it would make them look. While we are subject to the laws of man, we are certainly not of the law. Even when we are not in a position to speak out about Christ, the way we live our lives before men should shout our messages loudly. In many cases, we will be expected to conform to things that go against the Gospel. It is those very things that will cause us to have to make tough decisions that will likely bring persecution. No matter what, we must live our truth out loud. In these times, we must continue to stand for righteousness, trusting that God will indeed give us the grace to endure.

PRAYER

Lord...Give me the boldness to proclaim who you are and the strength to endure what may come because I do. In Jesus' name, Amen.

DAY SIX:
LET HIS WISDOM SPEAK

But the Spirit gave Stephen such wisdom that when he spoke, they could not refute him. ~Acts 6:9 (GNT)

AFFIRMATION
Today...I will hold my peace, speaking only what and when He leads me to speak on His behalf.

JUST A THOUGHT

In a time when many will come against the God that you profess, you only need to rely on Him to give the words to speak. So often people rise up to debate and defend the word of God when it is not necessary to do so. I have my own stance on this. We are not called to debate the Word; we are called display it. Speaking out of turn only causes people to further turn away from the things of God. But when we rely on Him to speak through us, we are more likely to cause doubters and naysayers to be drawn to Him.

PRAYER

Lord...Give me such wisdom, that when I speak, no one can deny how real You are in my life. In Jesus' name, Amen.

DAY SEVEN:
THE MATTER OF SOULS

"Look!" he said. "I see heaven opened and the Son of Man standing at the right side of God!"
~Acts 7:56 (GNT)

They kept on stoning Stephen as he called out to the Lord, "Lord Jesus, receive my spirit!" He knelt down and cried out in a loud voice, "Lord! Do not remember this sin against them!" He said this and died.
~Acts 7:59-60 (GNT)

AFFIRMATION
Today...I will be souls-focused rather than self-focused.

JUST A THOUGHT

While Stephen had every right to ask God to punish his murderers, he used his last moments to cry out to God on their behalf instead. When is the last time you asked God to bless your enemy? When is the last time you asked God to pardon those who knowingly came against you? When is the last time you asked God to hold back His hand of judgment against those who deserved to be punished? Let today be the day that you determine that you will judge the actions of others as God would instead of by your own standards for vindication. Allow God to contend with those who contend with you. This is His specialty.

PRAYER

Lord...May I see my enemies through your eyes and not my own. In Jesus' name, Amen.

DAY EIGHT: YOUR VOICE IS NECESSARY

Philip went to the principal city in Samaria and preached the Messiah to the people there. The crowds paid close attention to what Philip said, as they listened to him and saw the miracles that he performed.
~Acts 8:5-6 (GNT)

AFFIRMATION

Today...I will boldly proclaim what He has spoken to me, go where He has sent me, and do what He has told me.

JUST A THOUGHT

It really is not a matter of whether people will receive us or not. Obedience is key to getting the job done. Philip knew he did not carry a message of popularity. Further, he knew it could cost him his life, just like it did others like Stephen. Yet, he preached the Messiah anyway. It was his boldness that caused the people to take notice of him. Had he held back, what would be the outcome? Who knows? Who cares? He did not shrink back; he went forth. As a result, he gained a captive audience to present the wonders of God to. Now...You got next!

PRAYER

Lord...Make me bold as a lion when it comes to presenting you to the world around me. In Jesus' name, Amen.

DAY NINE: YOUR USED TO DOES NOT MATTER

Ananias answered, "Lord, many people have told me about this man and about all the terrible things he has done to your people in Jerusalem...The Lord said to him, "Go, because I have chosen him to serve me, to make my name known to Gentiles and kings and to the people of Israel.
~Acts 9:13; 15 (GNT)

AFFIRMATION

Today...I will walk in my new identity and will not allow anyone to judge me for the sins of my past.

<u>JUST A THOUGHT</u>

Just as God was transforming Saul and highlighting him as one He would use greatly to win souls for the Kingdom, his past was called into question. Ananias' first response when God sent him to Saul was to point out all that he had heard from others about his past transgressions against the people. Not much has changed since those times. People do the same thing today. As soon as some see elevation and promotion hit your life, they begin to question it, and even try to point out your flaws to people of influence. But as in the case of Ananias against Saul, God does not change His mind about blessing you because of the case others make against you; not even that of Satan, the accuser of the brethren. Once He has made up His mind to promote you, who you once were and what you once did does not even matter.

<u>PRAYER</u>

Lord...Thank You for overlooking who I was so that You could highlight who You created me to be. In Jesus' name, Amen.

DAY TEN: JUST CALL ME CORNELIUS

He was a religious man; he and his whole family worshiped God. He also did much to help the Jewish poor people and was constantly praying to God. It was about three o'clock one afternoon when he had a vision, in which he clearly saw an angel of God come in and say to him, "Cornelius!" He stared at the angel in fear and said, "What is it, sir?" The angel answered, "God is pleased with your prayers and works of charity, and is ready to answer you.
~Acts 10:2-4 (GNT)

AFFIRMATION

Today...I will do whatever it takes to get Heaven to respond to me.

JUST A THOUGHT

You just gotta love Cornelius. This man not only had a good reputation in his family but also among his community. He had clout in heaven too. His actions were so intentional and pleasing to God, that He sent an angel directly to Cornelius to let him know that he had gotten His attention. When is the last time you prayed a prayer that would move heaven and earth? When is the last time you served in a way that made God eager to respond to you? It is time that Christianity become more than just a label, but rather a status that carries weight in the heavens. As children of the Most High God, it should be a norm to experience Him employing angels constantly to show up on behalf of His people...as with Cornelius.

PRAYER

Lord...Give me the spirit of Cornelius; who was a good man who served Your people well and had a habit of prayer. In Jesus' name, Amen.

DAY ELEVEN: IT'S FOR ME TOO

And when I began to speak, the Holy Spirit came down on them just as on us at the beginning..."It is clear that God gave those Gentiles the same gift that he gave us when we believed in the Lord Jesus Christ; who was I, then, to try to stop God!"
~Acts 11:15; 17 (GNT)

AFFIRMATION

Today...I expect God to pour out His Spirit upon me, just as He did with the apostles of old; and of the new too.

<u>JUST A THOUGHT</u>

I have encountered men and women of God who present themselves as though they are God's only gift to the world. They act as though God is selective in who He can and will use to do great things in the Kingdom of God. It is as though their Bible reads differently than that of others. I assume theirs must omit the verse that says God is no respecter of persons. What is even worse is that many buy into this, worshipping them as idols. However, God is raising up a people who know they are anointed and called by Him. The same Spirit that was upon the apostles in the days of old is still being poured out today. Newsflash: It is not for a select few.

<u>PRAYER</u>

Lord...May I walk in the power of the Holy Spirit as those who have so before me. In Jesus' name, Amen.

DAY TWELVE:
HE IS SERVING UP SUDDENLY BREAKTHROUGHS

Then Peter realized what had happened to him, and said, "Now I know that it is really true! The Lord sent his angel to rescue me from Herod's power and from everything the Jewish people expected to happen."
~Acts 12:11 (GNT)

AFFIRMATION
Today...I expect to have an abundance of startling suddenly breakthroughs to come for me!

<u>JUST A THOUGHT</u>

There are those times that God causes steady but slow-moving progress toward certain breakthroughs we need. Nonetheless, it is not His intent for us to remain stagnant, not experiencing His best for our lives. Sometimes we get so use to what is that we just endure. Then there are times that we can come to a point of acceptance and complacency in the state we are in. God wants to rescue His people from that place. Oftentimes it is at that point that God can then come in and show Himself strong and mighty on our behalf...SUDDENLY, to the point it catches us completely off guard, just like when He delivered Peter from the prison.

<u>PRAYER</u>

Lord...May You suddenly interrupt not the just the plan of the enemy to take me out, but my own plan to camp out where You did not place me because of familiarity. In Jesus' name, Amen.

DAY THIRTEEN: PREACH AGAINST THE GRAIN

For this is the commandment that the Lord has given us: 'I have made you a light for the Gentiles, so that all the world may be saved.'...But the Jews stirred up the leading men of the city and the Gentile women of high social standing who worshiped God. They started a persecution against Paul and Barnabas and threw them out of their region. The apostles shook the dust off their feet in protest against them and went on to Iconium. The believers in Antioch were full of joy and the Holy Spirit.
~Acts 13:47; 50-52

AFFIRMATION

Today...I will remain true to my calling even if it upsets all of hell.

<u>JUST A THOUGHT</u>

Paul and Barnabas, as well as many of the greats in the Bible, were not favored by the people of the religious system. The goal was to silence them by any means necessary. You see, the religious system is in favor of what is popular as opposed to what is right. Whenever someone goes against what those of this mindset holds to be law, they get angry, and even devious at times. It is in these very experiences that those who are called by God must know full well who they are in Him. And when all of hell attempts to shut you down and shut you up...say what He says anyway!

<u>PRAYER</u>

Lord...Anoint me with the boldness of a lion to do what You say to do and to say what You tell me to say. In Jesus' name, Amen.

DAY FOURTEEN: PRESERVE YOUR OIL

In Lystra there was a crippled man who had been lame from birth and had never been able to walk. He sat there and listened to Paul's words. Paul saw that he believed and could be healed, so he looked straight at him and said in a loud voice, "Stand up straight on your feet!" The man jumped up and started walking around.

~Acts 14:8-10

AFFIRMATION

Today...I will pour into vessels that are not leaky, and who believe in who I am and value what I carry.

JUST A THOUGHT

I once heard a message titled "Don't Waste Your Oil", that completely changed my thought process concerning ministry. Over the years I have wasted a whole lot of time pouring into people who either do not believe that God can change them...or they just flat out do not really want change. Truth is, you can counsel, encourage, pray and prophesy until the Kingdom of heaven comes. Notice Paul was moved to minister to the man when he looked upon him and saw that he believed. Here's the deal...If people do not have faith, or just simply do not mind living in the state they are in, your labor of love will be in vain. Save your energy and your oil!

PRAYER

Lord...Help me to discern those You send my way for me to minister to; and redirect those who just want attention instead of awakening. In Jesus' name, Amen.

DAY FIFTEEN: EMBRACE SEASONS OF EXODUS

Barnabas wanted to take John Mark with them, but Paul did not think it was right to take him, because he had not stayed with them to the end of their mission, but had turned back and left them in Pamphylia. There was a sharp argument, and they separated...
~Acts 15:37-39 (GNT)

AFFIRMATION

Today...I will release anyone who is not part of my destiny.

<u>JUST A THOUGHT</u>

As humans, we are relational beings. Letting go of people is one of the greatest challenges we face sometimes. We do need people to survive, right? We do need people to form teams, right? We do need people to accomplish much of what God has given us to do, right? "Yes" is the answer to all of these questions. However, there is something that we must consider. We do not just need people to help us do what God has for us to do. We need the right people. Taking the wrong crew with you into your destiny is certain to cause an unnecessary derailment. It is best to embrace the notion of releasing those who do not belong with you. They are just hogging the spot that the right people need to slide into anyway.

<u>PRAYER</u>

Lord...Help me to know who to hold on to and who to cut loose. In Jesus' name, Amen.

DAY SIXTEEN: PRAISE THAT SETS MORE THAN YOU FREE

About midnight Paul and Silas were praying and singing hymns to God, and the other prisoners were listening to them. 26 Suddenly there was a violent earthquake, which shook the prison to its foundations. At once all the doors opened, and the chains fell off all the prisoners.
~Acts 16:25-26 (GNT)

AFFIRMATION

Today...I will praise as though not just my life, but the lives of others depend on it too.

JUST A THOUGHT

It is very easy to be self-focused when life comes against us, and we simply want to overcome whatever hardships we are facing. Paul and Silas were locked up in a prison wrongfully. Yet, they did complain. Instead, they prayed and sang praises unto God. Not only did God show up for them, but the other prisoners were set free as well. Even the guard and his family received salvation. Their story should be a reminder that what we face from day to day is not always just about us. Further, our response to our circumstances could result in not just our breakthrough, but that of others as well.

PRAYER

Lord...Keep me reminded that my weapon of praise could be someone else's key to freedom too. In Jesus name, Amen.

DAY SEVENTEEN: LET NO ONE MESS UP YOUR GOOD THING

[From Thessalonica]...the believers sent Paul and Silas to Berea. When they arrived, they went to the synagogue. The people there were more open-minded... They listened to the message with great eagerness, and every day they studied the Scriptures to see if what Paul said was really true. Many of them believed; and many Greek women of high social standing and many Greek men... But when the Jews in Thessalonica heard...they came there and started exciting and stirring up the mobs. 14 At once the believers sent Paul away to the coast...
~Acts 17:10-14 (GNT)

AFFIRMATION

Today...I am sticking with what I know instead going with the opinions of men.

JUST A THOUGHT

As Paul, Silas and Timothy preached from place to place; only a small percentage in the cities received them well...that is until they got to Berea, after having escaped the wrath of the Thessalonians. What is crazy to me is that the people of Berea knew full well that what Paul was preaching to them was Truth, as they had studied for themselves to prove it. However, when the Thessalonians came and stirred up riots, they wanted nothing more to do with Paul. They wanted him out. It is baffling to me, that they let outsiders come in and mess up their good thing. We can learn from this, to not do as they did in Berea. If you got a good thing going, do not toss it out, keep it going.

PRAYER

Lord...Help me to always make Your truth my own truth, such that I would not be swayed by the way another thinks. In Jesus' name, Amen.

DAY EIGHTEEN: THEIR IGNORANCE IS NOT YOUR ISSUE

When they opposed him and said evil things about him, he protested by shaking the dust from his clothes and saying to them, "If you are lost, you yourselves must take the blame for it! I am not responsible. From now on I will go to the Gentiles."
~Acts 18:6 (GNT)

AFFIRMATION

Today...I will not be affected by other people's choices that cause them to fall short of God's grace.

<u>JUST A THOUGHT</u>

Surely, just like Jesus, we would love to see all receive salvation and not be lost. However, we cannot force feed salvation or deliverance to people who flat out are not interested in receiving it. Our place is to be obedient in preaching the gospel, and presenting ourselves as witnesses for Him. However, we are not expected to take on the role of the receiver on behalf of those we are witnessing to. When we are not received, or the words we speak fall on deaf ears, we simply have to let the people own their own ignorance; as opposed to taking it personally as though we missed the mark.

<u>PRAYER</u>

Lord...Enable me to preach with conviction that does not allow me to compromise based on how others perceive me. In Jesus' name, Amen.

DAY NINETEEN: BUT WHO ARE YOU IN THE SPIRIT REALM?

God was performing unusual miracles through Paul... Some Jews who traveled around and drove out evil spirits also tried to use the name of the Lord Jesus to do this... But the evil spirit said to them, "I know Jesus, and I know about Paul; but you—who are you?"
~Acts 19:11; 13; 15 (GNT)

AFFIRMATION

Today...I will increase my influence in the realm of the Spirit by increasing my pursuit of the Father.

JUST A THOUGHT

There's nothing like showing up at a party or event where no one knows who you are. It is one thing to show up and quietly blend in, and another to try to gain attention for yourself. The latter could bring embarrassment at best and a beat down at worst. In Acts chapter 19, the seven sons of Sceva tried to gain notoriety based on who they knew or had heard of. That got them thrashed and thrown out. Here's a lesson concerning the need to establish a solid foundation in the spirit realm, not just so you can know God. You want all of hell to be very aware of who you are too.

PRAYER

Lord...Let me be so intentional about getting to know You, that Satan's kingdom will be very aware when it encounters me. In Jesus' name, Amen.

DAY TWENTY: A MATTER OF LIFE OR DEATH

And now, in obedience to the Holy Spirit I am going to Jerusalem, not knowing what will happen to me there. I only know that in every city the Holy Spirit has warned me that prison and troubles wait for me. But I reckon my own life to be worth nothing to me; I only want to complete my mission and finish the work that the Lord Jesus gave me to do, which is to declare the Good News about the grace of God. ~Acts 20:22-24 (GNT)

AFFIRMATION

Today...I will witness as though the lives of others depend on it, even if it costs me my own.

<u>JUST A THOUGHT</u>

In all actuality, in many ways it seems preaching the Gospel has become this glorified thing where people are rated by their presentations of it. In some circles and churches, it has become more about a program than people's salvation. Many even leave their gathering places of worship for preferential reasons--things that do not meet their standards personally, as opposed to considering the sinner who stumbled in next to them and is badly in need of salvation. The same is true outside the four walls of the church. Some never witness or disciple others because of the fear of how they will be viewed by others. It is time that we see each soul as Jesus does, and be willing to make the sacrifice He, and even Paul, did...even being willing to face death so that others can experience eternal life.

<u>PRAYER</u>

Lord...I want to be bold enough to preach Your Good News to any and everyone who needs it, no matter the cost. In Jesus' name, Amen.

DAY TWENTY-ONE: HOW TO COMMAND THE COMMANDER'S ATTENTION

The mob was trying to kill Paul, when a report was sent up to the commander of the Roman troops that all of Jerusalem was rioting. At once the commander took some officers and soldiers and rushed down to the crowd. When the people saw him with the soldiers, they stopped beating Paul. The commander went over to Paul, arrested him, and ordered him to be bound with two chains. Then he asked, "Who is this man, and what has he done?"
~Acts 21:31-33 (GNT)

AFFIRMATION
Today...I expect God to show up BIG for me!

<u>JUST A THOUGHT</u>

In doing what God has commissioned us to do, the risks are somewhat unpredictable. But we have them nonetheless. As with Paul, we have to keep forging ahead, trusting that we have a mighty deliverer and a God who has the ability to rescue us in the time of need. Just when your back is against the wall, He will always step...or at least send someone to your aide to do so. Trust that when you are marked as one of His, you will always be able to command His attention, just in time. Like Paul, at the brink of death, the very one who was in authority stepped in and called a cease movement. And though he ordered that Paul be arrested, he just had to know who this guy was.

<u>PRAYER</u>

Lord...May I always be positioned such that you can see me, and send those who will rescue me. In Jesus' name, Amen.

DAY TWENTY-TWO: FRIENDS WHO GO THE DISTANCE WITH YOU

The men with me saw the light, but did not hear the voice of the one who was speaking to me. I asked, 'What shall I do, Lord?' and the Lord said to me, 'Get up and go into Damascus, and there you will be told everything that God has determined for you to do.' I was blind because of the bright light, and so my companions took me by the hand and led me into Damascus.
~Acts 22:9-11 (GNT)

AFFIRMATION
Today…I will choose true friends, those who will go the distance with me.

JUST A THOUGHT

We are living in a day and time when loyalty seems so rare that it could almost be considered a commodity. To accomplish great things for God, we could certainly do it alone with Him. But it is so much better with friends, those who share the same heart for the Great Commission of Jesus Christ. Plus, the Bible tells us that one can chase a thousand; and two can put ten thousand to flight. So, I say we should go for the gusto. When selecting friends, co-laborers in the Gospel, measure their allegiance, reliability and trustworthiness. True friends, those whom God sends you, knows that sometimes they may not hear what you hear or see what you see. But when you need them, they will help get you to where you need to go anyway.

PRAYER

Lord…Send me friends who understand what it means to be loyal; so that we can, together, turn the world upside down for Your glory. In Jesus name, Amen.

DAY TWENTY-THREE: HE ALWAYS PROTECTS THE SENT ONE

And when I was informed that there was a plot against him, at once I decided to send him to you. I have told his accusers to make their charges against him before you."The soldiers carried out their orders. They got Paul and took him that night as far as Antipatris. The next day the foot soldiers returned to the fort and left the horsemen to go on with him. They took him to Caesarea, delivered the letter to the governor, and turned Paul over to him. The governor read the letter and asked Paul what province he was from. When he found out that he was from Cilicia, he said, "I will hear you when your accusers arrive." Then he gave orders for Paul to be kept under guard in the governor's headquarters.
~Acts 23:30-35 (GNT)

AFFIRMATION
Today…I will rely on my Father's covering as I walk out my mandate to operate in miracles, signs and wonders.

<u>JUST A THOUGHT</u>

Persecution is a part of the process for those who intend to do great things for God. The world's system, as well as the religious system, is not too keen on seeing the spiritual gifts go forth in the earth. Many still believe that it was for then and not for now. As with Paul, it will sometimes not be enough to try to muzzle you. Many will want to annihilate you for doing what God has called you to do. However, you must continue to walk in the same boldness, might and strength as Paul did. Stand firm in what God has mandated you to do. Do not back down...EVER. Just when the perfect plot has been planned against you; God will send a rescuer to protect you.

<u>PRAYER</u>

Lord...May I stand boldly, doing what you have called me to do...even in the face of opposition. In Jesus' name, Amen.

DAY TWENTY-FOUR: WHAT WILL YOUR CONFESSION BE?

I do admit this to you: I worship the God of our ancestors by following that Way which they say is false.
~Acts 24:14 (GNT)

AFFIRMATION

Today…I make my confession one that expresses adoration, praise and thanksgiving to my God!

<u>JUST A THOUGHT</u>

There are churches I have personally attended who advertise their Sunday morning gatherings as worship services. However, the part of the service designated as praise and worship seems rather restricted. There are rules surrounding how people should act, all in the name of being sensitive to those who are seeking. Now, I was under the impression that we are should all seek after the King of kings and Lord of lords, who is no doubt worthy of all praise, which should be shouted from a rooftop. Our expression of praise and worship should make bold declarations, not be a hidden part of who we are. I like Paul's audacity, to proclaim, even in the face of death threats, that he is a worshipper of the One his captors deny.

PRAYER

Lord...I want my life as a worshipper as a reflection of my never-ending faith in You.

DAY TWENTY-FIVE: STAND YOUR GROUND

Paul said, "I am standing before the Emperor's own judgment court, where I should be tried. I have done no wrong to the Jews, as you yourself well know. If I have broken the law and done something for which I deserve the death penalty, I do not ask to escape it. But if there is no truth in the charges they bring against me, no one can hand me over to them. I appeal to the Emperor."
~ACTS 25:10-11 (GNT)

<u>AFFIRMATION</u>

Today…I will stand firm on my convictions of my personal integrity as well as the truth concerning the Gospel, even if it costs me EVERYTHING.

JUST A THOUGHT

It is one thing to stand firm on the word of God and another to have your word not mean anything at all. People who are called to change the world must ensure to live a life that is above reproach. When accusations come, you should be able to refute them. When Satan, the accuser of the brethren, begins to make claims against you before God, you should be able to deny them. Paul was not at all hesitant in saying to the charges made against him, that there was no truth in any of the claims. We, too, should be able to do the same. Clean hands are those that are used to lay hands on the sick and see them recovered.

PRAYER

Lord…Help me to live my life in alignment with Your word, that I can easily walk out Your plan, purpose and will for my life. In Jesus' name, Amen.

DAY TWENTY-SIX: BOLDLY PROCLAIM WITHOUT SHAME

As Paul defended himself in this way, Festus shouted at him, "You are mad, Paul! Your great learning is driving you mad!"Paul answered, "I am not mad, Your Excellency! I am speaking the sober truth. King Agrippa! I can speak to you with all boldness, because you know about these things. I am sure that you have taken notice of every one of them, for this thing has not happened hidden away in a corner. King Agrippa, do you believe the prophets? I know that you do!"
~Acts 26:25-27 (GNT)

AFFIRMATION
Today…I will not back down from what I know to be the truth, and I will challenge others to own their truth as well!

<u>JUST A THOUGHT</u>

Ever encountered people who will change their story to win the popular vote or to fit in with the crowd? It is unnerving, to say the least. If you are not careful, you could find yourself caving, as well, to fit other people's molds just to fit in. The miracles done by Jesus ruffled lots of feathers. Paul's journey of boldness did the same. However, neither of the two tried to fit the status quo. Miracle workers are not those who back down when things heat up. They do not dance around the fire. They jump right in the middle of it.

<u>PRAYER</u>

Lord…I will never deny You or the great work You did on the Cross. I will preach until they cannot help but hear it. In Jesus' name, Amen.

DAY TWENTY-SEVEN: NOT ON MY WATCH

But now I beg you, take courage! Not one of you will lose your life; only the ship will be lost. For last night an angel of the God to whom I belong and whom I worship came to me and said, 'Don't be afraid, Paul! You must stand before the Emperor. And God in his goodness to you has spared the lives of all those who are sailing with you. So take courage, men! For I trust in God that it will be just as I was told. But we will be driven ashore on some island."
~Acts 27:22-26 (GNT)

AFFIRMATION

Today...I am taking full responsibility to all those God has entrusted to me for guidance, leadership and safety.

JUST A THOUGHT

While Paul and those traveling together were in the ship and were facing trouble, he knew he had to be the anchor, the stabilizer. Oftentimes we are put in the position of having to maintain peace, even in the midst of life's storms. When others are looking to you for the appropriate reaction, as a leader, you must be sober-minded enough to respond well. Functioning in the power of God can get a bit dicey at times. Those with you will look for guidance on how to navigate when the waters are troubled. When you stand firm on the promise of God, it gives them the courage to do the same.

PRAYER

Lord…Let my stance be so secure, that others will know and trust that standing with me is a place of stability. In Jesus' name, Amen.

DAY TWENTY-EIGHT: YOU WILL BE THEIR SIGN

Paul gathered up a bundle of sticks and was putting them on the fire when a snake came out on account of the heat and fastened itself to his hand. The natives saw the snake hanging on Paul's hand and said to one another, "This man must be a murderer, but Fate will not let him live, even though he escaped from the sea."But Paul shook the snake off into the fire without being harmed at all. They were waiting for him to swell up or suddenly fall down dead. But after waiting for a long time and not seeing anything unusual happening to him, they changed their minds and said, "He is a god!"
~Acts 28:3-6 (GNT)

AFFIRMATION
Today…I will not just show a sign of, but will be THE sign that Jesus is real!

<u>JUST A THOUGHT</u>

As Christians, our greatest call is to win others to Christ. That is not going to happen by beating them over the head with the Bible, offering them prayer each time we encounter them or by condemning them to hell because they do not believe as we believe. People are looking for a tangible sign that this God we profess is real indeed. It is our responsibility to show them how real He is. It is time that we begin to walk in signs, wonders and miracles to show people that we may be a tangible example of what God has the ability to do for them, the lost. We are all the sign that the world needs.

<u>PRAYER</u>

Lord…Cause me to rise to the occasion and become the sign of the times, making an impact in the lives of those who still need to know that You are their God. In Jesus' name, Amen.

ABOUT THE AUTHOR

YOLANDA PERRY is an emerging prophetic voice in this hour. She is the author of *GO!*; *Worth the Wait;* and several e-books including a series of Focused Fasting guides. Yolanda has served in all facets of ministry, to include leading women's ministry for five years; also ministering at the Washington State Corrections Center for Women for over ten years, where she led hundreds to salvation and witnessed many lives being transformed.

Yolanda served 11 years in the US Army. She holds academic degrees in concentrations, such as Business Administration/Accounting, Education, and Ministry & Church Leadership. But she is most proud to be a continual student of School of the Holy Spirit.

Currently, Yolanda is aligned with Ryan LeStrange Ministries & TRIBE Network under the leadership of Apostle Ryan LeStrange. Yolanda also serves as the lead intercessor of RLM Prayer Shield. She is also committed to her local assembly, Eastpointe Church in Bonney Lake, WA.

As a gifted speaker and writer, Yolanda's personal mission is to communicate and demonstrate unshakable faith. She currently writes inspirational messages and blogs on her Facebook, other social media channels and website, www.yolandaworldwide.com. She has been privileged to travel nationally and internationally carrying the Gospel of Jesus Christ around the world, fulfilling God's mandate that she would go to and that God would give her nations.

Now that Yolanda has fully embraced the charge to GO, you will see and hear much of her through her writings in books, audio and live messages, and throughout all social media outlets. She is also launching into new territories as an entrepreneur, beginning with the launch of her Ready. Set. GO! INTENSIVE (Mentorship Program); webinars, live broadcasts, and more.

Yolanda is the proud mother of three biological children, countless bonus kids through foster care, and is a beloved Nonnie to her beautiful grandkids.